BEER

© Food Editore
an imprint of Food Srl
Via Mazzini, 6 - 43121 Parma
Italy
www.foodeditore.it

ISBN 9788861543324

BEER

30 TASTY RECIPES
AND MUCH MORE

FOOD EDITORE

CONTENTS

BEER AROUND THE WORLD

Beer has a very long history. Throughout the millennia, this drink has remained essentially unchanged, an alcoholic beverage derived from the fermentation of cereals or grains.

The beer we drink today has very little in common with that drunk by the ancient Sumerians and Egyptians. There is, however, a link that connects the ancient beverage with what we recognize as beer today; it is the widespread appeal of this global beverage. Beer is probably the most commonly produced beverage on the planet.

But what exactly is beer? If we were to answer with a metaphor we could say that beer is like a house whose roof rests solidly on four supporting walls: water, barley malt, hops and yeast. Then there are the additional ingredients that make the world of beer both fascinating and complicated. There are a wide variety of brewing styles that enhance the creative possibilities of brewers the world over. Increasingly, fruit, nuts, and spices are used in many combinations to modify and enhance basic flavors; some combinations include cherries and raspberries, a range of spices, flowers and tobacco, chestnuts and peaches.

Creating a legend

The actual beer production process begins when the malt reaches the brewery. It starts off with the grinding of the grains that are then placed in a cauldron containing water. The mixture obtained is referred to as mash and is stirred constantly. The mash is kept at a temperature between 95°F (35°C) and 167°F (75°C). In smaller productions, the mashing process takes place in "onion" shaped copper containers, while in larger scale productions stainless steel tanks are used. In this phase the sugars contained in the ground malt dissolve in the water and, thanks to added yeasts, are converted into alcohol.

Once this first phase is completed, the obtained mixture, known as wort, is filtered and moved to a second cauldron where it is boiled with the hops.

Depending on the type of beer being made, hops may be added and cooked several times. The boiling phase continues in the cauldron for several hours. The lengthy cooking time is needed to dissolve some of the bitter elements in the hops and to sterilize the wort.

At this point the wort is ready for the yeast, which can be derived from previous fermentation or from the addition of pure yeast cultures cultivated in the brewery.

The yeast triggers a primary fermentation that produces alcohol and can last for about a week in a temperature-controlled environment. Low fermentation beers require a temperature around 50°F (10°C) while high fermentation beers need a temperature around 68°F (20°C). The first stage of production is often referred to as "turbulent" due to the large quantity of carbon dioxide released. The carbon dioxide causes the wort to simmer and at the end of this stage the beer is ready for maturation; also called seasoning or secondary fermentation.

In the maturation phase, the yeast is recovered, then the tanks are resealed to allow the carbon dioxide to incorporate into the beer, and the temperature is gradually lowered to 32°F (0°C).

7

The maturation of the beer can vary in length, but normally after four to six weeks the beer is ready to be filtered and transferred to bottles or kegs. While filtering is common for larger scale, industrial productions some types of beer are left unfiltered. Belgian blanches, Bavarian Hefeweizen and certain traditional British ales are characteristically unfiltered.

The big breweries also use the technique of pasteurization, a process used to eliminate microorganisms that takes its name from the French scientist Louis Pasteur.

In the process, special machines are used to quickly heat the kegs or bottles to an elevated temperature. This eliminates bacteria, usually still active yeast cells, which may be in the beer.

Many small, craft beer producers skip the pasteurization process, preferring to make a product that is, in a certain sense, "alive." It is a way to create a unique product that distinguishes them from large-scale producers.

To each his own

The next logical step in an explanation of beer would be a classification. This could be done by geographical origin, but here we have decided to make an initial, threefold division according to the type of fermentation process that occurs when the wort is transformed into finished beer.   All beers are fermented and can be grouped into three large families defined by type of fermentation: spontaneous, high and low. Dividing beer into these three groups also gives a chronological explanation of how beer has developed. The first beers were fermented spontaneously as the nature and function of the yeasts were unknown. With time, high fermentation beers developed. Such beer could only be made when brewers had gained full understanding of the process. Finally low fermentation beers came into production as the result of using more recently discovered yeasts, capable of "working" at lower temperatures. It should be kept in mind that there are numerous examples modern brewers employing all three types of fermentation.

9

SPONTANEOUS FERMENTATION

Beers with a long history that should be approached with an open mind, in order to best enjoy their unique flavors.

BEERS	DESCRIPTION
Lambic	Alcohol level around 5%, aged in barrels for around 1 year
Gueuze	Mix of two lambics of different ages

• Lambic

Lambic is the beer that, in many ways, best resembles the first beers. Traditional Lambic is produced in Belgium, specifically, in the limited area crossed by the Zenne River, called Pajottenland. The area is located southwest of Brussels, although some historic producers,

like the well-known Cantillon, have breweries on the outskirts of the Belgian capital. This extraordinary type of beer is produced by mixing barley malt and raw non-malted wheat (by law at least 30%). The hops used are aged for as long as two or three years so that they lose much of their aroma and the certain bitter characteristics. The ingredients provide for some characteristic flavor, however the truly distinctive feature of Lambic is its spontaneous fermentation. Traditional Lambic is only produced during the coldest months of the year.

It has an alcohol content of around 5%, and features truly unique aromas which are not always easy for the inexperienced consumer to understand. Lambic can be left for more than a year in the kegs, as a rule, up to two years, in order to obtain more complex aromas. These aged Lambics are most often used in assembling mixes.

• Gueuze

Gueuze, like Kriek, Framboise and Faro beers, is in a certain sense a Lambic "derivate". Gueuze, often called "Belgium's Champagne", is obtained by mixing two or more Lambics of different ageing. Gueuze is usually considerably more "fizzy" and has more complex flavors than Lambic. Like Lambic, traditional Gueuze is an extraordinary example of the infinite nuances that one can come across on the world beer scene.

HIGH FERMENTATION

This group seems to be more of a "world" than a category as high fermentation beers are many and widespread. They can be found from Belgium to Britain, as well as in France, Germany and many of the countries in between.

BEERS	DESCRIPTION
Altbier	Low alcohol level, amber, aromas of malt
Sticke	Similar to Altbier, but higher alcohol level (around 6.5%)
Kölsch	Fruity aromas, dry and slightly bitter
Gose	Very unusual, seasoned with coriander and salt
Berliner weisse	Marked acidity, low alcohol level (3.5%)
Weisse	Often has aromas of banana, cloves, liquorice and coffee
Ale	Large Anglo-Saxon family, opposed to the common "beer"
Barley wine	Very alcoholic, with complex, rich and intense aromas
Irish red ale	Can offer both the sweetness of malt and the bitterness of hops
Porter	Very dark beer, easy drinking and low in alcohol
Stout	Dry and light-tasting, with a bitter aftertaste
Abbey	One of the most complex and varied families
Trappist	Certified, made only by eight European breweries
Saison	Light, thirst-quenching beer, pleasantly bitter
Blanche	Low alcohol level, with coriander and bitter orange spicing
Oud bruin	An unique taste balanced between sweet and sour
Bière de garde	Beer for aging, with fruity, malted notes

• Altbier

A German beer typical to Düsseldorf and the surrounding areas, Altbier (literally "old beer") takes its name from the "old" high fermentation technique. It usually has a limited alcohol content, a fine amber color and recurring aromas that recall malt and caramel and leave a pleasantly bitter aftertaste. Diebels Alt and the Hannen Alt are among the most popular brands.

• Sticke

This Düsseldorf beer's name means "secret". The beer is, in fact, virtually unknown outside the German city. In some way it is similar to an Altbier, although it has a higher alcohol content, 6.5% as opposed to 5%.

• Kölsch

The traditional beers from the city of Cologne are better known than some other German beers. They too have a long history, dating back to the fourteenth-century. Kölsch beers offer a delicate fruity aroma, a dry and slightly bitter flavor that makes them easy to drink. Best-known brands include Kupper Kölsch and Gaffel Kölsch.

• Gose

A great rarity, Gose beers are from Saxony, specifically the area on the outskirts of Leipzig. These wheat beers are flavored with coriander and, surprisingly, salt. The resulting beer has a pale-yellow color and an unusual sour taste of lactic acid, which is even striking to some Lambic drinkers.

• Berliner weisse

Not to be confused with the more famous Bavarian Weisse. By law, and as stated in the name, Berliner Weisse is made only in Berlin. This is a wheat and barley malt beer, whose fermentation, thanks to a very special yeast mix that includes the aforementioned Brettanomyces bruxellensis, gives strong acidity.

This beer has a very low alcohol content not exceeding 3.5%, and is considered cool and refreshing. It is traditionally served with a shot of cordial that can be either green (milkweed based), or red (made of raspberries). Beyond providing a hint of color, the added cordial has the purpose of mitigating the acidity of the beer. The most famous brand of Berliner Weisse is Kindl Weisse.

• Weisse or Weizen

The Weisse or Weizen beer is a symbol of Bavaria, a region of Germany with an important brewing tradition and the host of the annual Oktoberfest. Weisse is produced with barley malt and a specific, char-

13

acteristic wheat variety. By law, at least half of the total grain used in Weisse must come from this particular wheat variety and it must be made with special yeast that gives it an aroma reminiscent of banana and cloves. There are several types of beer that fall into the Weisse category. The most well known and widely available is Hefeweizen. It is uniquely unfiltered and is characterized by its cloudy or opalescent appearance. Kristallweizen might be the opposite of Hefeweizen, as it is filtered and is clear in appearance. Dunkel Weizen beer is made with dark roasted malts and has aromas that tend toward coffee and licorice. Finally, there is the stronger Weizenbock, with an alcohol content that can exceed 7%. It is generally more complex and structured. Several brands are available including labels from the old Weihenstephan brewery, the popular Erdinger or Oberdofer as well as Paulaner and Aynger brands, just to name a few.

• Ale

This name identifies a large and complex family of beers (many British) that can be distinguished by the traditional high fermentation process used in production. As previously mentioned there are several different types of ale. Mild ales, which have a low alcohol content, are often dark in color and have a typical caramel flavor. The most popular and widespread ales are, undoubtedly, the bitter ales. The bitter flavor is the result of being hopped with the Fuggle and Goldings hops varieties. These ales also have a low alcohol content. A bitter rarely exceeds 4%, and is characterized by the intense fruity notes and for easy drinkability. In regions outside of the UK, often times in continental Europe, Best or Special bitters are available. These ales are slightly more alcoholic, around 4.5%, the Extra Special Bitter is known for being among the strongest of the dark ales.
The category also includes pale ales that, despite the name, are gener-

ally amber-colored and have an alcohol content of around 5% and a particularly bitter and refreshing aftertaste. Among the classics are Bass Pale Ale, made famous by its appearance in a famous painting by French impressionist painter Manet, and Whitbread Pale Ale; popular American brands include Sierra Nevada Pale Ale and Liberty Ale made by the Californian Anchor Steam brewery.

Indian pale is an historic ale that was traditionally produced for British soldiers in the colonies, specifically in India. This ale has made a recent comeback on the international beer-drinking scene. Examples include the Anglo-Saxon style Marston India's Export and Deuchars IPA. There are similar style pale ales being made in the US, but they are generally referred to as American pale ale. More restricted geographically, at least in Britain, is brown ale, characterized by its brown color and a characteristic hint of hazelnut, followed by notes of caramel.

Heading further north into Scotland, the so-called Scotch ales are prominent. They are dark in color, often with ruby reflections. Scottish ales also stand out because they have a slightly sweeter malt flavor and higher alcohol content. They are generally classified according to their alcohol content into Light, Heavy, Export and Strong categories, but one still sees the old classification. 60/-, 70/-, 80/- and 90/- shillings, corresponding to the taxes paid in sterling.

While the Scottish Ales tend to be more alcoholic than their English relations, England comes into its own with its old ale; a beer particularly suited to aging, usually dark, alcoholic, with a rich, fruity and vinous aroma. The most common labels include Old Tom Robinson, Greene King Strong Suffolk and Theakston Old Peculiar.

• Barley wine

Also British in origin, this unique beverage is a part of the vast category of ales. Barley Wines have a high alcohol content (easily exceeding 10%) and are complex, rich and intense beverages. Undoubtedly the most famous British brands are Thomas Hardy's Ale and George Gale Old Prize Ale. In the U.S. Anchor Steam produces the well regarded the Old Floghorn.

17

• Irish red ale

Ireland is correctly considered the motherland of stout, but its amber beers cannot be forgotten. Almost all the big companies produce ales, but some small Irish microbreweries are emerging as the top producers in this category. Flavors and aromas may vary, but for the most part the focus of these beers is to enhance either the sweet or bitter flavor of the malt. Well-known brands include Murphy's Irish Red, Mc Farland Red and Kilkenny Irish Beer.

• Porter

It is said that a pub landlord in London created porter in 1772. At the time, it was common for pub patrons to order an "Entire" or a "Three Threads". These drinks were a mixture of three different beers, the least expensive and lightest beer, the full-bodied ale and the most expensive beer in the bar. The result was pleasing and allowed customers to save a few pennies. However, having the drink mixed to order was a lengthy process and required a bit of a wait. So, Ralph Harwood, the owner of the well-known bar, decided to mix three types of beer before they were ordered and the Porter was born. This beer takes its name from the typical clientele of Harwood's pub, the porters working in the area. Porter is a very dark beer, easy to drink and with low alcohol content, flavors include hints of coffee, prunes and dried fruit.

• Stout

Stout is one of the better-known beers due, in part, to the widespread popularity the Guinness brand. Guinness is a dry stout that was produced for centuries by the Guinness family. In 1759 Arthur Guinness first began making his stout in Ireland. Others followed him and some of the most popular brands include Beamish Irish and Murphy's Irish stout. These dark, rich beers are favorites of many beer drinkers around the globe.

The high fermentation stouts are dark in color and have a beautiful ruby reflection when held up to the light. Their characteristic aromas include coffee, licorice and smoke. The flavor is it is dry, light and with a very pleasing hint of bitterness at the end. Within the stout category there are several variations. The sweet or milk stout is one uncommon example that is still produced in small quantities. Milk stout is different from the dry Irish stout as it is sweetened with lactose. This gives flavors of milky coffee and chocolate. Oatmeal stout, a more common variation, is made with oats. The use of this cereal produces a deep, multifaceted aroma and a less bitter, more palatable flavor. Imperial stout is alcoholic, complex and compelling. It is also known as Imperial Russian as this beer had great success in the nineteenth century at

the czar's court. Its alcohol content is around 8% by volume and it has a bouquet spanning from coffee to chocolate, from boiled prunes to licorice. Modern brewers are experimenting with flavor combinations in stouts; one of the most successful is the chocolate and coffee stout which is distinguished by its distinctive chocolate and coffee flavors.

19

• Abbey

The so-called "Abbey beers" are defined by the producer and not necessarily the production method, as the beers within this group are stylistically diverse. The common thread for these beers is that they can trace their history back to a specific abbey. Many are now produced in modern, non-religiously affiliated breweries following a recipe handed down from the original abbey producers. In fact most of the abbey beers, unlike the Trappist beers, are produced outside the monastery walls and sometimes the image of a friar or the word abbey are nothing more than a very successful marketing ploy. Therefore, among the abbey beers we find products which vary greatly in terms of color, aroma, taste and alcohol content. The most famous labels, many of which are distributed by international beer companies, are Affligem, Leffe, Floreffe, and Grimbergen.

• Trappist

Trappist beers are quite famous and have a very limited production. In fact, there are only eight breweries in the world that can claim to make an authentic Trappist product. Six of these are located in Belgium, Orval, Chimay and Rochefort are in the Wallonia, while Westmalle, Vestvleteren and Achel are in Flanders. The seventh brewery, "the Trappe," is located in Holland and, after some initial difficulties, it has been accepted into the Trappist ranks. The last brewery is in Austria. These beers can be vastly different from one another, from the light Blond produced at Vestvleteren to the bitter and unique Orval. Rochefort and Westmalle beers have high alcohol content and a complex flavors. Beer experts and industry professionals regard the Trappist beers as some of the most valuable.

• Saison

The name means beers of the "season". These beers originated in the Hainaut region in Belgium as light, refreshing and pleasantly bitter beverages. They were particularly well suited the lifestyle of the time, as they gave farmers and fieldworkers refreshment and nutrients throughout the day. Modern Saison beers are slightly stronger, about 7%, and are available year around as they have become more and more commercially successful over time. The most well known of these beers are Saison Dupont, la Saison 1900, la Saison de Silly and la Saison de Pipaix, produced in the historic Brasserie a Vapeur owned by Jean Louis Dits.

• Blanche or Witbier

The "white" beers from Belgium are called blanche if produced in the French-speaking Wallonia and witbier if produced in the Flemish-speaking Flanders. These beers have a low alcohol content, about 5%, and are produced with malted barley and a small percentage of un-malted wheat. The unique flavor of these beers comes from the spices, which can include coriander and bitter orange peel, and the lack of filtering. As unfiltered beers, they are characteristically cloudy, like Hefeweizen, with its yeast sediments. The best known and most readily available are Hoegaarden, Wieckse Witte, Brugs Witbier, Blanche de Namur and Blanche de Bruxelles.

21

• Oud Bruin

Oud Bruin is a lesser-known, highly fermented Belgian style beer. These beers come from the area around eastern Flanders and their colors vary from intense amber to dark brown with a ruby reflection. They are characterized by their unique flavor that ranges from sweet to sour. The most famous Oud Bruin brand is Rodenbach from Roeselare.

• Bière de garde

Originating in the northeastern part of France along the Belgian border, Bière de Garde is an aged beer, traditionally produced in spring and stored, thanks to its elevated alcohol content, until the following summer. Bière de Garde is characterized by flavors that hint of fruit and malt. The best-known brands are 3 Monts from Brasserie Sylvestre, Jenlain from Duick and Bière du Ch'ti from Castelaine.

LOW FERMENTATION

This is the most modern of the fermentation styles. It is the defining technique for lagers and consequently it dominates global production.

• Pils

This type of beer has revolutionized the modern market. Its name comes from Pilsner Urquell, which was produced for the first time in 1842, in the Bavarian town of Pilsen. It's a golden colored beer, enriched by the extraordinarily full aroma of the local hops, well-known variety called Saaz. Traditionally Bavarian-style brewing produces a clear beer characterized by herbaceous aromas, the soft, elegant taste of malt and a final touch of bitterness. Well known examples include, Pilsner Urquell, Staropramen and Budweiser Budvar. The pils produced in Germany and Austria generally have a stronger hops flavor. Due to the large German beer production, there are plenty of well-known German brands: from Becks to Warsteiner, from Kulmbacher to Bitburger.

Belgium pils have a more delicate aroma and flavor. There are several famous examples of Belgian pils, including Stella Artois, Jupiler, Maes and Silly Pils. The Netherlands produces a number of well-known pils that are widely available around the world, including Heineken, Ams-

23

BEERS	DESCRIPTION
Pils	A light beer with characteristic hoppy accents
Dunkel	Lagers with toasted malt, including the important Schwarzbier
Bock	Full-bodied beer with a well-defined malt flavor
Dortmunder	Pale beer, in the past considered more "rustic" than Pils
Lager	Light beer with well-balanced aroma and flavor

tel, Grolsch, Brand and Bavaria. Carlsberg, Tuborg and the Royal from the brewery Ceres dominate the Danish market.

Pils is found almost everywhere: other examples include Kronenbourg in France, Cardinal in Switzerland, San Miguel and Cruzcampo in Spain, Efes in Turkey and Marathon in Greece.

• Dunkel

Dunkel is the name given to the German toasted malt lagers. The most important of this category are called Schwarzbier (black beer), which have a hint of chocolate and coffee flavors. Augustiner Dunkel and Alpirsbacher Dunkel are important Dunkel labels and Kapuziner Schwarze and M␣nchshof's Schwarzbier are among the better-known Schwarzbier brands.

• Bock

This type of beer probably originated in the German town of Einbeck. Bocks are full-bodied with a distinct taste of malt. If the alcoholic degree is 6.5% or lower it still considered bock, and if the alcoholic degree is above 7%, it is a doppelbock. Both beers are full-bodied, well structured and are characterized by caramel and honey notes and with an emphasis on the soft, lingering aftertaste. The doppelbock frequently have hints of roasted flavors. There are many well-known brands available; Maibock from Augustiner brewery and Spaten Premium Bock are great examples of bocks. The doppelbocks often have names ending in –ator, like Paulaner Salvator, Celebrator from Aynger and Optimator from Spaten.

• Dortmunder

Dormunder is the typical beer from Dortmund, located in the north-western region of Germany. It was initially made in the middle of the nineteenth century and was considered more "rustic" than the pils. Over the years this clear-colored beer has been refined to suit consumer tastes. The best-known example is the Dab brand.

• Lager

The term lager can extend across the entire family of low-fermentation beers. It is the largest of the categories due to the wide reaching success of the product and also the number and size of the breweries producing this variety. Lager is a light, moderately alcoholic beer characterized by the notable equilibrium between malt and hops. It is pleasant to drink and pairs well with many different types of food, making it well suited for many occasions.

GLASSES

Beer enthusiasts who have had the opportunity to visit a well-stocked pub or a brewery will have realized that there is a wide variety of beer glasses: from the classic pint glass to the handled mug, from the simple cylindrical glass to goblets that are vaguely reminiscent of mediaeval drinking vessels. Particularly strong beers, like many abbey varieties, Trappist and barley wine, should be served in large glasses (6) which help to decant and oxidize the intense aromas and better taste the structure. Weizen, on the other hand, should be served in tall narrow glasses. Nearly all bars, pubs and restaurants now serve weizens in a tall glass that is narrow for most of its height and widens slightly at the top (7). This type of glass is important because it conserves the froth, allowing it to remain even after the initial sips. In Great Britain and Ireland pint glasses are always used (5). The glasses have a truncated conical shape that allows for the dispersion of carbon nitrogen and enables the distinctive "fall" of the thick head that is characteristic of many British beers.

Pils should be served in high, narrow fluted glasses (3), which help the characteristic head. Blanche on the other hand are normally served in simple large glasses (9), which aid in releasing the citrus and spice

notes in these beers; thicker glasses will help to maintain the low temperature at which blanche should be served. Finally the classic mug (1-2) is fine for low fermentation beers, even if it could easily be replaced by the tulip glass (8). The German altbier are normally served in simple cylindrical glasses (4).

TEMPERATURE FOR SERVING

It is a common misconception that beer should be served cold. The optimal temperature varies greatly depending on the type of beer. Excessive cold can inhibit the aromas and flavors and deprive the consumer of some of the tastiest characteristics of the beer.

TYPE OF BEER	TEMPERATURE
Low fermentation beers (lager, pils, etc.)	about 42.8°F (6°C)
Blanche, weizen type beers	46.4-48.2°F (8-9°C)
Full bodied beers (bock, doppelbock)	50°F (10°C)
Structured and alcoholic beers (abbey, trappist, etc.)	53.6°F-57.2°F (12-14°C)

How to Recognize
and Taste a Good Beer

LOOK

Once poured in the glass, the beer should be evaluated for foam quality, transparency and color.

Let's start with the foam. Though it is true that almost all beers should be presented with a **head of foam**, it is worth knowing that **for some types, the foam is almost non-existent**. This is the case with barley wines and some other unusual beers, often with very high alcohol levels. **What's important is that the foam is fine and compact**, without large bubbles, which are almost always the result of a mistake during tapping. Quality beers keep their foam until the glass has been drained, leaving traces on the glass which the Belgians poetically call "Brussels lace." These traces are a clear sign that the glass has been correctly washed, without the use of chemical detergents.

Moving down, we can observe the beer's color and transparency. Most beers are filtered, in which case limpidity or even brilliance are essential, though this is not the case for beers that are unfiltered, as are many artisanal brews. **As for color, which primarily depends on the type of malts used, the chromatic spectrum for beers is very wide**. They can range from a pale straw yellow, which often reveals the use of malts from grains other than barley, to brilliant amber, orange or copper tones, up to beers that are brown or even darker, with ruby hints or an impenetrable blackness.

SMELL

When you bring the glass of beer up to your nose, the first thing to do is to **concentrate on the two great categories of scents found in beer, from the malt and from the hops**.

From the malt, we can often detect notes that recall honey, usually acacia honey for pale beers and chestnut honey for darker beers. These aromas can be of greater or lesser intensity, which is another

variable to assess. The fragrance of the hops manifests itself as notes of freshly cut grass or citrus fruits like mandarin or grapefruit, obviously depending on the type, or types of hops.

Other aromas that are easy to find come from the type of malt used: The toasted malts used for dark stouts, for example, always bring hints of chocolate, cacao and licorice.

TASTE

The best thing to do during this delicate phase is to **take a mouthful of beer, not a small sip as when tasting wine or especially spirits**, but trying, without overdoing it, to allow the beer to wet the entire tongue. As is commonly known, different parts of the tongue can sense different flavors, so the first mouthful helps to distinguish the intensity and quality of these different tastes.

Sweetness, which recalls in a more subtle way the sweetness of honey, comes mostly from the malt. Saltiness is almost nonexistent in beers, except for some exceptional cases like gose.

Acidity, though it can seem a defect, is a fundamental requirement and very pleasant in certain beers, for example the slightly citric sensation of certain weizen.

Finally, bitterness. **It is a cliché that beers are bitter**, so much so that in certain cases some present it as though it was a defect. The word itself can sometimes be a hindrance. The intensity and quality of bitterness in beers can vary greatly, but it is a highly enjoyable bitterness, and perhaps the most distinctive trait of authentic beers. Some beers have a barely hinted-at bitterness while in others the bitter dominates from start to finish, leaving a long lingering memory on the palate.

MADE with beer

BEER-BATTERED
Anchovies

SERVES 4

2 cups (1 lb or 500 g) fresh anchovies · 2 eggs
1/3 cup (2 oz or 50 g) all-purpose flour
1/2 cup (3 ½ fl oz or 1 dl) Pils beer
vegetable oil for frying · 2 tbsps white wine vinegar
1 garlic clove, minced · parsley, minced
salt and pepper

Remove the heads, the bones and the entrails from the anchovies. Wash carefully and leave to dry on a paper towel. Beat the egg yolks in a bowl, sift in the flour and add the beer a little at a time. Beat the egg whites until firm, and carefully fold them into the mixture, season with salt and pepper.

Heat abundant vegetable oil in a deep frying pan. Dip the anchovies into the batter and coat completely. Transfer the battered anchovies to the hot oil and fry until golden brown. Work in batches so as not to overcrowd the pan.

Using a slotted spoon, transfer the anchovies to a paper-towel lined plate. When the excess oil has been absorbed, move the anchovies to a serving dish and sprinkle over the vinegar, chopped garlic and parsley. Let stand for about an hour and serve at room temperature.

Preparation time
30 minutes

Cooking time
10 minutes

Skill level
easy

Serve with
Pils

Variation

A lighter version of this dish can be made by simply dredging the anchovies in flour and pan frying. Serve the anchovies immediately, seasoned with fresh lemon juice.

SAVORY
Potato Tarts
with Bacon

SERVES 4

1 onion, thinly sliced · 4 tbsps extra-virgin olive oil
4 white potatoes, peeled and diced
1 ¼ cups (10 fl oz or 3 dl) Lager beer · 4 tbsps breadcrumbs
4 slices bacon · 3/4 cup (5 oz or 150 g) sour cream · mustard · salt

Preheat the oven to 400°F (200°C). Heat the olive oil in a large frying pan and add the onions. Sautee until the onions begin to brown and add the potatoes. Toss the potatoes and onions together in the pan and let cook for a few minutes. Pour over the beer and cook until tender. Mash the potatoes with a fork. Season with salt.

Spoon the mixture into 4 oiled ramequins and top each one with 1 tbsp breadcrumbs. Bake for 15 minutes or until golden brown.

Meanwhile, fry the bacon until crisp. Mix the sour cream and mustard together to form a smooth sauce. Unmold the potato tarts and serve with the bacon and mustard sauce.

Preparation time
10 minutes

Cooking time
20 minutes

Skill level
easy

Serve with
Lager

Variation
Substitute the bacon in this recipe with the same amount of speck.
For added spice, add freshly ground pepper to the mashed potatoes.

MADE with beer

CHICKEN
Liver Pâté

SERVES 4

1 shallot, minced · 1/2 cup (4 oz or 100 g) butter
1 bay leaf · 1 ¾ lb or 800 g chicken livers
1 ¼ cups (10 fl oz or 3 dl) Pils beer · 2 sheets of gelatin
1 loaf crusty French bread, sliced and toasted · 1 clove garlic
salt and pepper

34

Heat 2 tablespoons butter in a large frying pan and add the shallots and bay leaf. Sauté briefly, add the chicken livers and season with salt and pepper. Pour over 1/3 cup (1 dl) of beer and let simmer until the liquid has evaporated and the livers are cooked through, about 35 minutes.

Remove the bay leaf. Melt the remaining butter, add to the chicken livers and blend until smooth. Heat the remaining beer until warm. Meanwhile, soak the gelatin in cold water for a few minutes. Drain and squeeze out any excess liquid. Add the gelatin to the beer and let dissolve.

Transfer the pâté to a bowl and pour the beer gelatin over the top. Cover and refrigerate overnight. Unmold the pâté and garnish with bay leaves. Toast the French bread and rub with the garlic clove. Serve the pâté with the garlic bruschetta.

Preparation time
20' + resting time

Cooking time
35 minutes

Skill level
easy

Serve with
Pils

Variation

For a more flavorful pâté, add juniper berries,
fresh thyme and dill before pouring into the mold.

MADE with beer

MUSHROOM
and Mashed Potato Gratin

SERVES 6

1 handful of dried mushrooms
1 cup (8 fl oz or 2,5 dl) Abbey beer
2 ½ lb (1 kg) white potatoes, peeled and diced
2 cups (14 fl oz or 4 dl) milk · 1/4 cup (2 oz or 50 g) butter
5 tbsps grated parmesan cheese · 1 garlic clove, finely sliced
2 tbsps extra-virgin olive oil
1 ½ cups (6 oz or 180 g) Mozzarella cheese, diced · salt

36

Preparation time
45' + resting time

Soak the mushrooms in the beer for 30 minutes. Boil the potatoes in the milk for about 30 minutes, drain, reserving a bit of the cooking liquid. Mash the potatoes together with the reserved cooking liquid, butter, parmesan and a pinch of salt. Preheat the oven to 350°F (180°C).

Cooking time
1 hour

Heat the olive oil in a frying pan and add the garlic. Sautee briefly, add the drained mushrooms and let cook for a few minutes. Remove from heat and add the garlic and mushrooms to the mashed potatoes. Stir in the diced Mozzarella. Transfer the mixture to a buttered baking dish and bake until golden-brown, about 20 minutes. Remove from the oven and serve warm.

Skill level
easy

Serve with
Abbey

Variation

The gratin may be prepared in layers: spread half of the potato mixture into a baking dish, top with a few slices of ham and cover with the remaining potato mixture. Bake as indicated above.

MADE with beer

GNOCCHI
with Sausage

SERVES 6

1 yellow onion, finely chopped
3 tbsps extra-virgin olive oil · 2 sage leaves
2 mild sausages, casings removed and chopped
1/2 cup (3 ½ fl oz or 1 dl) Lager beer
1 lb (500 g) prepared potato gnocchi, salt and white pepper

Bring a large pot of salted water to a boil and add the gnocchi. Let cook for 5 minutes.

Meanwhile, heat the olive oil in large frying pan. Add the onions and sage and sauté for a few minutes. Add the sausage meat and brown quickly. Add the beer and cook over high heat for a minute. Reduce heat and cook until most of the liquid has evaporated.

Drain the gnocchi and add them to the hot sausage ragù. Toss in the pan to coat and season with freshly ground white pepper. Serve immediately.

Preparation time
20 minutes

Cooking time
15 minutes

Skill level
easy

Serve with
Lager

Variation
You can also use this tasty ragù to top pasta:
try it with penne or farfalle.

MADE
with beer

LINGUINE
with Octopus
and Green Beans

SERVES 4

*2 ¼ lb (1 kg) octopus · 1 red onion, possibly Tropea variety
1 bay leaf · 10 white peppercorns
3 tbsps extra-virgin olive oil · 1 clove garlic, minced
2/3 cup (5 fl oz or 1 ½ dl) Blanche beer
1 cup (3 ½ oz or 100 g) green beans, washed and trimmed
14 oz (400 g) linguine · salt*

Wash the octopus under cold running water. Place the octopus, red onion, bay leaf and peppercorns in the pot and bring to a boil. Cook for 1 hour and 30 minutes. Remove the octopus from the pot and reserve the cooking water. Once cool, cut the octopus into bite-sized pieces.

Meanwhile, cook the green beans in boiling salted water for about 7 minutes. Drain and chop. Heat the olive oil in a large frying pan and add the garlic, let cook briefly. Add the octopus and the beer and cook until half of the liquid has evaporated. Add the green beans and toss to coat.

Bring the reserved cooking liquid to a boil and cook the linguine until "al dente". Drain, add the pasta to the hot octopus and toss to coat. Serve immediately.

Preparation time
20 minutes

Cooking time
110 minutes

Skill level
easy

Serve with
Blanche

Variation

For a thicker sauce, boil one diced potato with the linguine. Drain and proceed with the above recipe.

PACCHERI
with Shrimp

SERVES 4

1 1/3 cups (11 fl oz or 3,3dl) Weisse beer
1/4 cup (2 ½ oz or 60 g) salt · 12 shrimp, shelled and deveined
1/4 cup (2 oz or 50 g) cane sugar · chives, chopped
white pepper · 2 red chili peppers
1 handful of mint leaves · 2 tbsps extra-virgin olive oil
13 oz (380 g) paccheri pasta

42

Mix the beer with the salt in a baking dish. Add the shrimp, cane sugar, chives and season with freshly ground white pepper. Cover and refrigerate. Let the shrimp to marinade for 12 hours. Blanch the chili peppers in boiling water to loosen the thin outer skin. Drain, cool under cold, running water and remove the skins and the seeds. Process the peppers and the mint in a blender.

Bring a large pot of salted water to a boil. Add the paccheri and cook until "al dente".

Meanwhile, drain the shrimp. Heat the olive oil in a large frying pan, add the shrimp and cook over high heat until translucent. Add the chili and mint paste and toss to coat. Add the drained pasta to the pan with the shrimp, toss to coat. Remove from heat and serve immediately. Garnish with chopped chives if desired.

Preparation time
20' + resting time

Cooking time
20 minutes

Skill level
easy

Serve with
Weisse

Variation

Replace the chives with finely chopped spring onion greens.
This sauce can also be used on short pasta like farfalle or penne.

CREAMY HERB
Risotto

SERVES 4

2 tbsps extra-virgin olive oil
1 shallot, minced · 1 ½ cups (10 oz or 280 g) Carnaroli rice
3/4 cup (7 fl oz or 2 dl) Pils beer
2 ½ cups (1 ¼ pint or 7 dl) boiling vegetable stock
1 bouquet of mixed herbs (arugula, borage, wild chicory,
chives), minced · 2 tbsps (1 oz or 30 g) butter,
2 tbsps grated parmesan · salt and white pepper

Preparation time
20 minutes

Cooking time
20 minutes

Skill level
easy

Serve with
Pils

Heat the olive oil in a deep frying pan. Add the shallot and cook until translucent. Add the rice and toast, stirring constantly, until it begins to smell nutty. Add most of the beer and let the alcohol cook off. Add the boiling stick by the ladleful, stirring and letting the stock absorb before adding more. After 10 minutes, stir in the chopped herbs.

Cook for a further 8-10 minutes, adding stock and stirring. When the rice is cooked and the risotto has reached the desired consistency, remove from heat and stir in the parmesan. Season to taste with salt and white pepper. Drizzle over the remaining beer and let sit for a minute before serving.

Tips and tricks

Borage, also known as starflower, is an herbaceous plant
that grows wild throughout Italy and the Mediterranean region.
Borage should be cooked before eating.

ROAST
Rack of Lamb

SERVES 4

2 racks of lamb, rinsed and dried
dry white wine · 4 tbsps extra-virgin olive oil
2 rosemary sprigs · 1 onion, diced · 1 celery stalk, diced
1 carrot, diced · 1/2 cup (3 ½ fl oz or 1 dl) vegetable stock
1/2 cup (3 ½ fl oz or 1 dl) Stout beer
1 tbsp all-purpose flour, sifted · salt and pepper

46

Marinade the lamb in the white wine for at least 2 hours. Remove the meat from the marinade and discard the wine. Heat 2 tablespoons of olive oil in a frying pan and sear the racks of lamb. Reduce heat add the rosemary sprig and cook for 25 minutes, turning twice. Remove from heat and season to taste with salt and pepper. Cover with foil and let rest for 5 minutes.

While the meat is cooking, prepare the sauce: heat the remaining olive oil in a frying pan and add the onion, celery and carrot. Mince the remaining rosemary sprig and add it to the onions. Sauté until the onions are translucent and then add the stock and the beer. Bring to a boil and reduce to half the original volume. Remove from heat, add the flour and carefully stir with a fork to break up any lumps.

Arrange the lamb on a platter and pour over the stout sauce. Serve immediately.

Preparation time
20' + resting time

Cooking time
25 minutes

Skill level
easy

Serve with
Stout

Variation
Serve the lamb with steamed
vegetables and fried sage leaves.

MADE with beer

WEISSE
Chicken

SERVES 4

4 tbsps (2 oz or 60 g) butter · 2 shallots, finely chopped
4 chicken thighs · 2/3 cup (5 fl oz or 1 ½ dl) Weisse beer
1 cup (7 oz or 200 g) blanched chestnuts
1 green apple, peeled and diced
fresh marjoram · pink peppercorns · salt and pepper

48

Heat 2 tablespoons of butter in a deep frying pan. Add the shallot and sauté until translucent. Add the chicken thighs and brown evenly on both sides. Season with salt and pepper and add half of the beer. Reduce the liquid by half and then add half of the chestnuts and half of the apple.

After 30 minutes add the remaining chestnuts, the remaining apple, a few marjoram leaves and the crushed pink peppercorns.

Cook for a further 10 minutes. Add the remaining butter to the pan to thicken the gravy. Serve hot garnished with fresh marjoram.

Preparation time
20 minutes

Cooking time
40 minutes

Skill level
easy

Serve with
Weisse

Variation

For a more flavorful dish, wrap the chicken thighs in a slice of bacon before cooking.

MADE with beer

ROASTED
Pork Shanks

SERVES 4

4 small pork shanks · 2 carrots, roughly chopped
2 onions, quartered · 1 celery stalk, roughly chopped
1 garlic clove · rosemary · 1 bay leaf
1/2 tsp dried coriander · black peppercorns
3/5 cup (7 fl oz or 2 dl) Abbey beer · salt

FOR THE SAUCE
2 cloves garlic, minced · 2 tsps honey
1/4 cup mustard · 1/4 tsp ground white pepper

Place the pork shanks in a pot with plenty of water. Add the carrots, onions, celery, garlic, herbs and spices and bring to a simmer. Reduce heat and simmer for 2 hours. Prepare the sauce: mix together the garlic, honey, mustard, season with salt and ground white pepper and stir until smooth.

Remove the shanks from the broth and pat dry with paper towels. Coat the shanks with the prepared sauce. Let to rest for about 1 hour. Preheat the oven to 350°F (180°C). Place the pork shanks in a roasting pan and pour over the beer. Bake for 1 hour. Serve with roasted new potatoes and garnish with fresh rosemary.

Preparation time
20' + resting time

Cooking time
3 hours

Skill level
easy

Serve with
Abbey

Variation
The honey may be omitted from the sauce for a spicier dish. Pair the pork shank with a side dish of boiled cabbage dressed with olive oil, vinegar, pepper, cumin. Top with sautéed onion and crispy bacon bits.

CRISPY
Squid Tempura

SERVES 4

1 lb (500 g) medium-sized squid
1 fresh ginger root, about 1 ½ inches (4 cm), peeled and grated
1 cup (5 oz or 150 g) rice flour
1/3 cup (2 oz or 50 g) all-purpose flour
1/2 cup (3 ½ fl oz or 1 dl) Saison beer
vegetable oil for frying · salt

Clean the squid, removing the bone and eye. Rinse and dry. Cut the squid into large pieces and place them in a dish. Sprinkle over the ginger, cover and let marinate for 3 hours.

Mix together the 2 types of flour and whisk in the cold beer. Dip the squid pieces into the batter to coat completely. Heat abundant vegetable oil in a saucepan. Working in batches, fry the squid pieces until golden-brown.

Use a slotted spoon to remove the squid and transfer to a baking rack lined with parchment paper. Season with salt, garnish with thinly sliced ginger and serve immediately.

Preparation time
20' +resting time

Cooking time
10 minutes

Skill level
easy

Serve with
Saison

Variation

The squid may be substituted with cuttlefish. For a mixed tempura plate, batter and fry a few pieces of zucchini sliced into matchsticks.

MADE with beer

APPLE
Fritters

SERVES 4

1 ¼ cups (6 oz or 160 g) all-purpose flour, sifted
5 tbsps sugar · 1/2 tsp salt · 4 eggs
1/2 cup (3 ½ fl oz or 1dl) milk
1/3 cup (3 fl oz or 0,8 dl) Weisse beer
3 apples, peeled and sliced · 1/4 cup (2 oz or 50 g) butter
1/2 tsp cinnamon · vegetable oil for frying

54

Mix together the flour, 2 tablespoons of sugar and the salt. And add the eggs and milk and mix well. Pour in the beer and whisk until smooth.

Heat the butter in a frying pan and sauté the apples with 1 tbsp sugar, until tender and caramelized. Let cool slightly and add to the batter, adding a spoonful of flour if the mixture is too thin. In a separate bowl mix together the remaining sugar with the cinnamon.

Heat abundant oil in a saucepan. Drop a spoonful of batter into the boiling oil, cook the fritter until golden brown and remove onto a drying rack lined with parchment paper. Continue frying the fritters until all of the batter is used. Roll the hot fritters in the cinnamon and sugar mixture and serve immediumtely.

Preparation time
20 minutes

Cooking time
15 minutes

Skill level
easy

Serve with
Weisse

Variation
Apple fritters may be served as a dessert
or as an accompaniment to savory pork dishes.

BEER
and Coffee Tiramisù

SERVES 4

1/4 cup (2 oz or 50 g) sugar · 3/4 cup (7 fl oz or 2 dl) Stout beer
3/4 cup (7 fl oz or 2 dl) strong coffee · 12 ladyfinger cookies
unsweetened cocoa powder · dark and milk chocolate flakes

MASCARPONE CREAM

1 ¼ cups (10 fl oz or 3 dl) whipping cream · 1/4 cup
(2 ½ oz or 60 g) room temperature mascarpone · 6 egg yolks
2/3 cup (4 oz or 120 g) sugar · 1/4 cup (2 fl oz or 0,6 dl) Stout beer

Preparation time
30 minutes

Whip the cream into stiff peaks, fold it into the soft mascarpone and refrigerate. Beat the egg yolks with the sugar until thick. Drizzle in the beer, a little at a time, and continue whisking until it has been absorbed into the mixture. Cook the mixture over a water bath, whisking continuously, for 10-15 minutes or until doubled in volume. Fold the egg mixture into the mascarpone mixture.

Cooking time
20 minutes

Dissolve the sugar in the beer in a saucepan; add the coffee and bring to a boil over medium heat. Cook for 5 minutes. Let cool and then soak the ladyfingers in the syrup. Line the bottom of 4 ramequins with a layer of ladyfingers. Top with a layer of mascarpone cream. Continue layering, finishing with a layer of mascarpone cream, until all of the ingredients are finished. Dust the top of each ramequin with cocoa powder and decorate with the chocolate flakes.

Skill level
medium

Serve with
Stout

Variation

For an original presentation of this coffee
and beer tiramisù, serve the pudding in glass beer mugs.

RAISIN-WALNUT
Cake

SERVES 4

1 1/3 cups (7 oz or 200 g) raisins
3 ¼ cups (14 oz or 400 g) all-purpose flour
3 tsps baking powder
1 tsp cinnamon
1 tsp vanilla · 3 tsps glucose syrup
1 1/3 cups (11 fl oz or 3,3 dl) Barley Wine beer
9 tbsps (4 ½ oz or 125 g) butter, softened
3/4 cup (3 oz or 75 g) walnuts, coarsely chopped · salt

Preparation time
15' + resting time

Soak the raisins in warm water for 30 minutes. Preheat the oven to 350°F (175°C).

Mix together the flour, baking powder, salt and cinnamon. In a separate bowl mix the glucose syrup with the beer and add the butter. Make a well in the center of the flour mixture and pour in the wet ingredients. Gently stir to form a smooth batter.

Cooking time
75 minutes

Drain the raisins and add them to the batter along with the walnuts. Pour the batter into a buttered, floured 9 ½-inches (24 cm) diameter baking dish. Bake for 1 hour 15 minutes. Remove from the oven and cool completely before serving.

Skill level
easy

Serve with
Barley Wine

Variation

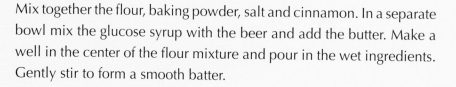

Try making a chocolate glaze for the cake: melt 11 oz (300 g) dark chocolate with 3/4 cup (7 fl oz or 2 dl) whipping cream in a double boiler. Pour the warm glaze over the cake and let stand for 15 minutes before serving.

FOCACCIA
with Pancetta

SERVES 4

1 cup (5 oz or 150 g) Italian pancetta (bacon), diced
1/3 cup (2 oz or 50 g) cornmeal
12 oz (350 g) prepared focaccia/pizza dough
3 tbsps extra-virgin olive oil
1 bunch of mixed aromatic herbs, minced · salt and pepper

60

Preheat the oven to 400°F (200°C). Knead 2 tablespoons of pancetta 2 tablespoons of cornmeal into the dough. Roll out the dough onto a 9 ½-inches (24 cm) diameter baking sheet, leaving the dough rather thick. Brush with oil and dust the surface with cornmeal.

Fill a spray bottle with water and spray the focaccia from about 12-inches (30 cm) away. Sprinkle a pinch of salt over the surface of the focaccia. Let rise for 20 minutes in a warm place.

Bake the focaccia for 25 minutes. Add the aromatic herbs and rest of the pancetta after about 15 minutes. Continue to bake until the pancetta is crispy and the fat rendered. Remove from the oven, season to taste with salt and pepper and cut into wedges.

Preparation time
20' + resting time

Cooking time
25 minutes

Skill level
easy

Serve with
Lager

Variation

For a complete meal, serve the focaccia
with a plate of steamed vegetables.

PIZZA
with Potatoes and Porcini

SERVES 4

2 tsps active dry yeast · 1 tsp sugar · 4 tbsps extra-virgin olive oil
4 cups (1 lb or 500 g) all-purpose flour · 2 tsps salt

TOPPING
extra-virgin olive oil · 3/4 cup (7 fl oz or 2 dl) tomato sauce
2 cups (7 oz or 200 g) fresh Mozzarella, diced
1 cup (7 oz or 200 g) smoked Provola cheese · 4 small potatoes
3 cups (9 oz or 250 g) porcini or portabella mushrooms,
cleaned and sliced · salt and pepper

Preparation time
40' + resting time

Pour the yeast into 1 cup of lukewarm water, sprinkle over the sugar and let sit until foamy. Mound the flour on a work surface and make a well in the center. Pour the yeast mixture into the well and add the olive oil and salt. Carefully mix to form a rough dough, adding more water if necessary. Knead until smooth and place in an oiled bowl. Cover with a clean kitchen towel and let rise until doubled in size, about 2 hours. Preheat the oven to 400°F (200°C).

Cooking time
30-35 minutes

Press the dough into 4 8 ½-inches (22 cm) oiled pizza pans. Spread the tomato sauce over the dough, top with the sliced Mozzarella and the provola. Bake for 15-20 minutes. Meanwhile, boil the potatoes; drain, peel and mash. Spread the mashed potatoes over the cooked pizza. Top with the mushrooms and season with salt, pepper and a little olive oil.

Skill level
easy

Serve with
Bock

Variation
Try replacing the mushrooms with 1 cup (7 oz or 200 g)
Italian pancetta crumbled over the pizza.

CACIOCAVALLO,
Bacon and Zucchini Rolls

SERVES 4

2 ½ tsps active dry yeast · 1 tsp sugar · 4 cups (1 lb or 500 g) all-purpose flour · 3 tbsps extra-virgin olive oil · 1 tbsp salt

FILLING
1 tbsp extra-virgin olive oil · 1 zucchini, cut into matchsticks 1/2 red pepper, diced · 1/2 yellow pepper, diced · 1 cup (4 oz or 125 g) bacon, diced · 2 ½ cups (9 oz or 250 g) shredded Caciocavallo or other aged cheese · oregano · salt and pepper

Preparation time
45' + resting time

Cooking time
40 minutes

Skill level
easy

Serve with
Pale Ale

Dissolve the yeast in a ¼ cup of warm water. Sprinkle over the sugar and let sit until foamy. Pour the yeast mixture over the flour and add the salt, oil and 1 cup (3 dl) water. Mix to form a dough and knead until smooth. Let rise until doubled in volume.

Preheat the oven to 350°F (180°C). Sauté the zucchini in the oil and season with salt and pepper. Roast the peppers in the oven for about 20 minutes. Place in a bag and let sweat for 20 minutes. Remove the skin and seeds and slice into strips. Punch down the dough and roll it out into a large rectangle. Spread the vegetables, cheese and bacon, over the dough leaving a ½-inch border. Season with oregano and roll up the dough lengthwise to form a log. Pinch the edge closed to seal. Let rise for 1 hour. Cut the roll into 1-inch slices and transfer to a parchment paper-lined baking sheet. Let rise for 1 hour. Preheat the oven to 350°F (180°C) and bake the rolls for 15 minutes.

Variation

For a more mild version, replace the Caciocavallo cheese with buffalo or cow's milk Mozzarella.

MARGHERITA
Pizza

SERVES 4

2 tsps active dry yeast
1 tsp sugar · 4 tbsps extra-virgin olive oil
4 cups (1 lb or 500 g) all-purpose flour · 2 tsps salt

TOPPING
4 tomatoes, peeled and pureed · 4 tbsps extra-virgin olive oil
2 cups (7 oz or 200 g) fresh Mozzarella, diced and left to drain
salt · basil

66

Preparation time
30' + resting time

Cooking time
20 minutes

Skill level
easy

Serve with
Pils

Dissolve the yeast in 1 cup of lukewarm water, sprinkle over the sugar and let sit until foamy. Mound the flour onto a work surface and make a well in the center. Pour the yeast mixture into the well and add the olive oil and salt. Carefully mix, adding more water if necessary, to form a rough dough. Knead until smooth and place in a large bowl. Cover with a clean kitchen towel and let rise until doubled in size, about 2 hours.

Preheat the oven to 400°F (200°C). Press the dough into 4 8 ½-inches (22 cm) oiled pizza pans. Spread the tomato sauce over the dough. Sprinkle over the salt and drizzle over some olive oil. Bake for 20 minutes, remove the pizzas from the oven, top with the Mozzarella and return to the oven. Bake until the cheese has melted. Top the pizzas with fresh basil and serve immediately.

Variation
**For a Caprese pizza, top the baked pizza
with quartered cherry tomatoes.**

POTATO,
Spinach and Asiago Quiche

SERVES 6

9 oz (250 g) prepared savory pastry dough
extra-virgin olive oil · 3 potatoes · 3 eggs
1/2 cup (3 ½ fl oz or 1 dl) whipping cream
2 tbsps grated parmesan · 1/2 tsp ground nutmeg
salt and pepper · 1 bunch of fresh spinach, washed and dried
3 cups (11 oz or 300 g) chopped Asiago
5 slices of ham · 1 tsp poppy seeds

Preheat the oven to at 375°F (190°C). Roll out the pastry dough and place in an oiled 9 ½-inches (24 cm) diameter pie pan. Pierce the dough with a fork and set aside.

Boil the potatoes in salted water until tender. Drain, peel and slice. Whisk together the eggs, cream, parmesan and nutmeg. Season with salt and pepper.

Layer the potatoes, spinach, Asiago cheese and ham into the pastry shell, starting with the potatoes. Pour over the egg mixture and sprinkle over the poppy seeds. Bake the quiche for about 45 minutes. Let cool completely before and serving.

Preparation time
75 minutes

Cooking time
65 minutes

Skill level
easy

Serve with
Abbey

Variation

Try substituting the Asiago with Mozzarella cheese and the spinach and ham with 4 cups portabella mushrooms sautéed with 1 garlic clove.

ONION
and Caprino Tart

SERVES 4

*2 tsps active dry yeast · 2 cups (9 oz or 250 g)
all-purpose flour · 1/2 cup (2 oz or 50 g) spelt flour
2 tbsps extra-virgin olive oil · salt*

FILLING

*4 onions, thinly sliced · 2 tbsps extra-virgin olive oil
3 tbsps Vin Santo (Italian dessert wine) · 3 slices white bread
1/2 cup (3 ½ fl oz or 1 dl) milk · 1 cup (4 oz or 120 g) fresh
Caprino (goat cheese) · salt and pepper*

Preparation time
30' + resting time

Cooking time
40 minutes

Preheat the oven to 375°F (190°C). Dissolve the yeast in 1/4 cup of lukewarm water and let sit for 10 minutes. Mix together the two types of flour, add the yeast mixture, oil, salt, and enough water to form a rough dough. Knead quickly to form a firm and smooth dough. Let rest for 20 minutes.

Heat the oil in a frying pan and add the onions; sauté for a few minutes and add the Vin Santo. Reduce the heat, cover and simmer for about 15 minutes. Remove from heat and let to cool. Soak the bread in the milk until soft. Squeeze out the excess liquid and crumble into a bowl. Add the cheese, cooked onions and season to taste with salt and pepper. Roll out the dough and set it into a parchment paper-lined a 9 ½-inches (24 cm) diameter baking dish. Add the onion filling and bake 25 minutes.

Skill level
easy

Serve with
Lager

Variation

Substitute the Caprino with the same quantity
of Ricotta for a more mildly flavored tart.

ABRUZZO-STYLE
Fettuccine

SERVES 4

3 tbsps extra-virgin olive oil
1 cup (5 ½ oz or 160 g) pancetta (bacon), diced
1 small onion, diced · parsley, chopped
basil, chopped · salt and pepper
12 oz (350 g) fettuccine · 1/4 cup (25 g) grated Pecorino

72

Bring a large pot of salted water to a boil and add the fettucine. Cook until "al dente".

Meanwhile, heat the oil in a large frying pan. Add the onions and pancetta and let brown. Remove from heat and stir in the parsley and basil. Season to taste with salt and pepper. Add a ladleful of pasta water to form a smooth sauce.

Drain the pasta and pour into the pan with the pancetta sauce. Toss the pasta and sauce in the pan over high heat. Remove from heat, drizzle with olive oil and finish with grated Pecorino and chopped parsley. Serve immediately.

Preparation time
10 minutes

Cooking time
15 minutes

Skill level
easy

Serve with
Lager

Variation

For a thicker sauce, sauté 1 cup (3 ½ oz or 100 g) cherry tomatoes with the onions and pancetta.

BAKED GNOCCHI
with Spinach and Emmental

SERVES 4

2 ¼ lb (1 kg) potatoes
2 cups (200 g) all-purpose flour nutmeg · salt

FILLING
12 cups (1 lb or 500 g) spinach, washed and drained
5 tbsps (2 ½ oz or 60 g) butter · 7 oz (200 g) mortadella, thinly sliced · 7 oz (200 g) Emmental cheese, thinly sliced · 2 cups (7 oz or 200 g) prepared ragù · 4 tbsps grated parmesan · salt

Preparation time
40 minutes

Cooking time
70 minutes

Skill level
medium

Serve with
Abbey

Steam the spinach, remove from heat and drain off any excess water. Melt the butter in a frying pan and add the spinach. Sauté for a few minutes and season with salt; drain well. Boil the potatoes in salted water until tender. Peel and pass through a potato ricer. Add the flour, salt and ground nutmeg and knead together to form a smooth dough. Lightly flour a work surface and roll out to a 1/2-inch thick rectangle.

Preheat the oven to 350°F (180°C). Place a layer of mortadella over the dough and then the Emmental. Top with the sautéed spinach. Roll the dough up like a jellyroll and place on a clean kitchen towel. Tie both ends of the towel tightly with kitchen twine. Boil the roll in salted water for 15 minutes. Drain and leave to cool. Unwrap and cut the roll into 1-inch thick slices. Butter a baking dish and pour in a layer of ragù. Layer in the gnocchi and top with the remaining ragù. Sprinkle over the parmesan and bake for 20 minutes.

Variation
Substitute the mortadella with the same amount of ham
and the Emmental with thinly sliced Scamorza.

RICE TIMBALE
with Sausage and Artichokes

SERVES 4

*1/4 cup (1/2 oz or 15 g) dried mushrooms · 5 tbsps
(2 ½ oz or 70 g) butter · 1 small onion, diced · 2 cups
(7 oz or 200 g) sausage, casings removed · 1/2 cup
(3 oz or 80 g) peas · 3 artichokes, trimmed, chokes removed
and sliced · 1/3 cup vegetable stock
2 ¼ cups (12 oz or 350 g) Italian long grain rice
1/2 cup (3 ½ fl oz or 1 dl) dry white wine
3 tbsps grated parmesan · salt and pepper*

Preheat the oven to 400°F (200°C). Soak the mushrooms in lukewarm water for 30 minutes. Drain, reserving the liquid, and set aside. Heat 1 ½ tablespoons butter in a frying pan and add the onion. Sauté briefly and crumble in the sausage. Add the peas, artichokes, vegetable stock and mushrooms. Simmer for 30 minutes over medium heat.

Boil the rice in salted water for 5 minutes, drain and add to the sausage and vegetable mixture. Add the remaining butter, white wine, grated parmesan, pepper, and 10 tablespoons of the reserved soaking liquid. Transfer the rice into a buttered casserole dish and bake for 10 minutes, stir the rice and continue baking for another 20-25 minutes. Remove from the oven, cut into slices and serve immediately.

Preparation time
30' + resting time

Cooking time
65 minutes

Skill level
easy

Serve with
Bitter Ale

Variation

This dish can be made in individual ramequins that have been buttered and coated with breadcrumbs.

PAPPARDELLE
with Rabbit Ragù

SERVES 4

1 rabbit, deboned and cut into 8 pieces
6 tbsps extra-virgin olive oil · salt and pepper
2 tbsps (1 oz or 30 g) butter · 1 onion, finely chopped
1 carrot, diced · 1 stick celery, diced
1/3 cup (2 oz or 50 g) Italian pancetta (bacon)
1/4 cup (2 fl oz or 60 ml) tomato sauce
1/2 cup (4 fl oz or 1 dl) vegetable stock
14 oz (400 g) pappardelle pasta

Preparation time
20' + resting time

Place the rabbit in a pan, drizzle over 2 tablespoons of olive oil and season with salt. Cover, refrigerate and let sit for 2 hours.

Bring the rabbit to room temperature and drain off any liquid. Heat the butter and 1 tablespoon of oil in a deep frying pan and brown the rabbit pieces. Add the onion, carrot, celery and the pancetta. Season with salt and pepper. Add the tomato sauce and stock. Cover and simmer for about 1 hour, adding more stock if necessary.

Cooking time
70 minutes

Bring a large pot of salted water to a boil and add the pasta. Cook until "al dente", drain and transfer the pasta to the rabbit ragù. Toss the pasta with the sauce to coat. Remove from heat and serve immediately.

Skill level
medium

Serve with
Strong Ale

Variation

This recipe can also be made with wild rabbits or other game. In this case, omit the tomato sauce and increase the pancetta to 1/2 cup (4 oz or 100 g).

PAIR
with beer

GRILLED
Frankfurters
with Sauerkraut

SERVES 4

2 heads of cabbage, thinly siced
2 tbsps white wine vinegar · 3 tbsps extra-virgin olive oil
1 tbsp honey · salt and pepper
12 small frankfurters · 3 tbsps sweet mustard

80

Bring a large pot of water to a boil. Add the vinegar and then the cabbage. Blanch for a few minutes. Drain the cabbage and cool under cold running water.

Preparation time
15 minutes

Dry the cabbage on paper towels or leave it to drain in a colander. Heat the olive oil in a large frying pan and sauté the cabbage over high heat.

Cooking time
10 minutes

Drizzle over the honey and season to taste with salt and pepper. Continue cooking until the cabbage is brown and crisp. Heat a cast iron grill pan and cook the sausages over medium heat, turning often, until browned and cooked through. Season with a little bit of salt, if desired, and serve with the sauerkraut and mustard.

Skill level
easy

Serve with
Weisse

Variation

This is a great dish for an Oktoberfest celebration.
Serve the sausages with Bavarian mustard and accompany
with fresh pretzels and Bavarian Rye bread.

ROAST PORK
with Grapes and Onions

SERVES 6

3 ½ lb (1 ½ kg) pork loin
12 slices smoked bacon · extra-virgin olive oil
1 cup (7 fl oz or 2 dl) dry white wine
12 small onions, thinly sliced
1 bunch of red grapes, washed, seeded and halved
4 laurel leaves · 3 cloves
4 juniper berries · salt and pepper

Wrap the bacon slices around the pork loin and tie with kitchen string. Heat 1 tablespoon of oil in a nonstick frying pan and brown the meat on all sides. When the roast is golden brown, pour over the wine and let the alcohol cook off. Reduce heat to low and add the onions and the grapes. Add the spices and season with salt and pepper.

Cover and cook over medium heat for about 2 hours, basting occasionally with the cooking liquid and adding water if necessary. Turn the meat over every 15 minutes to prevent it from sticking to the pan. Mash the grapes with a fork to release the juices. When the roast is cooked through remove from the pan and let cool slightly. Remove the string and slice. Discard the laurel, the juniper berries and the cloves, pour the sauce over the roast and serve.

Preparation time
20 minutes

Cooking time
135 minutes

Skill level
medium

Serve with
Abbey

Variation

For a classic pork roast, replace the onions with diced new potatoes and cook together with the meat.

CRISPY
Fried Rabbit

SERVES 4

1 rabbit, deboned and cut into 8 pieces
4 garlic cloves, peeled and finely sliced · 4 rosemary sprigs
2 tsps freshly ground nutmeg · 2 tbsps all-purpose flour
3 eggs, beaten · salt · extra-virgin olive oil

84

Rinse and dry the rabbit pieces. Pound with a meat tenderizer to flatten slightly. Place the rabbit pieces in a baking dish and add the garlic, rosemary and ground nutmeg. Stir to coat, cover and refrigerate. Marinate for 6 hours.

Dredge the rabbit in the flour. Beat the eggs with a pinch of salt and ground nutmeg. Heat the oil in a frying pan. Working in batches, dip the rabbit in the egg mixture and fry, turning once, until golden-brown on both sides.

Transfer the rabbit to another hot frying pan, cover and finishing cooking the rabbit over low heat. Remove the rabbit from the pan transfer to a paper towel-lined plate for a few minutes. Sprinkle with sea salt and serve with a mixed green salad.

Preparation time
30' + resting time

Cooking time
20 minutes

Skill level
medium

Serve with
Pils

Variation

The recipe can also be made using chicken tenders. Pair the dish with a sauce made from equal parts of mustard and low-fat plain yogurt seasoned with toasted slivered almonds and salt.

PAIR with beer

ONION
Frittata

SERVES 6

8 cups (2 ¼ lb or 1 kg) red onions, thickly sliced
4 tbsps extra-virgin olive oil · 4 eggs
4 tbsps grated parmesan · salt and pepper
parsley, finely chopped

86

Heat 2 tablespoons of olive oil in a large frying pan and add the onions. Cook until soft and remove from heat. Pour off any liquid and let cool completely.

Whisk the eggs in a bowl, add the grated parmesan, salt, pepper and the finely chopped parsley. Add the onions and mix well. Heat the remaining olive oil in a large frying pan, pour in the onion and egg mixture and reduce heat to low.

When the bottom of the frittata is golden-brown and the top is set, flip and cook for a few more minutes. Allow to cool slightly before serving. Cut into wedges and garnish with parsley and red onion.

Preparation time
10 minutes

Cooking time
20 minutes

Skill level
easy

Serve with
Pale Ale

Variation

For a unique flavor, replace the parmesan with
the same quantity of Caciocavallo cheese.

PAIR with beer

BAKED
Potatoes with Cheese

SERVES 4

4 large baking potatoes
2 ¼ cups (9 oz or 250 g) mild Cheddar cheese, shredded
1/2 cup (3 oz or 80 g) butter · salt and pepper

Boil the potatoes in salted water until tender, about 35 minutes. Drain and cool slightly. Slice the top of the potato open and use a spoon to loosen the skin a little. Preheat the grill.

Top the potatoes with the cheese and then the butter. Wrap the base of each potato in aluminum foil and place on a baking sheet. Grill for 5 minutes or until the cheese has melted and has formed a crispy crust. Season to taste with salt and pepper and serve.

Preparation time
10 minutes

Cooking time
40 minutes

Skill level
easy

Serve with
Lager

Tips and tricks

Cheddar, a typical English cheese, is traditionally aged for 3 months. Mild Cheddar has a smooth flavor and a mild scent.

PAIR
with beer

POLENTA
with Spare Ribs and Sausages

SERVES 6

4 cups (1 lb or 500 g) cornmeal for polenta · salt
3 ½ oz (100 g) pork throat meat · 1/2 lb (500 g) sausage, chopped
1 lb (500 g) pork spare ribs · 1 cup (8 oz or 250 ml) dry white wine

Bring 8 ½ cups (2 liters) water to a boil in a large pot. Season with salt and pour in the cornmeal in a thin stream, whisking constantly. When all of the cornmeal incorporated reduce heat to low and continue stirring with a wooden spoon. Cook for 45 minutes.

In a large pan, brown the pork throat meat, sausage and spare ribs; season with salt and pour over the wine. Continue cooking over medium heat for 1 hour, adding water if necessary.

Transfer the polenta to a serving dish and make a well or a hole in the center. Pour the braised meat into the center and serve immediately. Garnish with parsley if desired.

Preparation time
5 minutes

Cooking time
1 hour

Skill level
easy

Serve with
Bock

Variation

The spare ribs and sausage may be
cooked on grill pan or the barbeque.

PORK
and Sausage
Meatballs

SERVES 4

1/2 cup (2 oz or 50 g) breadcrumbs
1/4 cup (2 fl oz or 60 ml) milk · 2 eggs
1 tbsp white wine vinegar · 14 oz (400 g) lean ground pork
3 ½ oz (100 g) sausage, casing removed · salt and pepper
2 leeks, washed and thinly sliced, white part only
1 tbsp cornstarch · 6 tbsps extra-virgin olive oil
1/2 cup (3 ½ fl oz or 100 ml) dry white wine
1 tbsp all-purpose flour · 1 bunch parsley, chopped

92

Preparation time
20 minutes

Mix together the breadcrumbs, milk, eggs, vinegar, pork, sausage, half of the leek and the cornstarch dissolved in a little water. Mix well and season to taste with salt and pepper.

Cooking time
20 minutes

Roll the mixture into walnut-sized balls. Heat the oil in a large frying pan and add the remaining leek. Add the meatballs and brown. Pour over the wine, cover and cook for 15 minutes. Stir in the flour to thicken the cooking juices. Serve the meatballs hot, garnished with chopped parsley.

Skill level
easy

Serve with
Pils

Variation
For a lighter dish, replace the pork
with ground chicken or turkey.

INDEX

PRINTED IN CHINA in January 2013

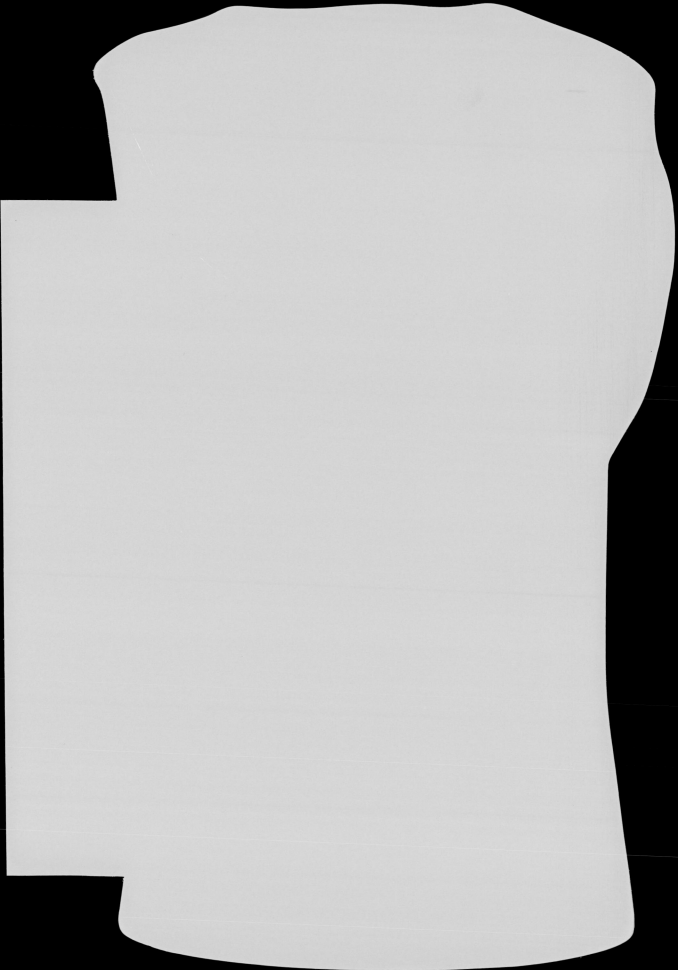